W9-AOT-422

a blessing of

peace

A BLESSING OF peace

WELLERAN POLTARNEES

LAUGHING ELEPHANT BOOKS MMI

ISBN 1-883211-40-9

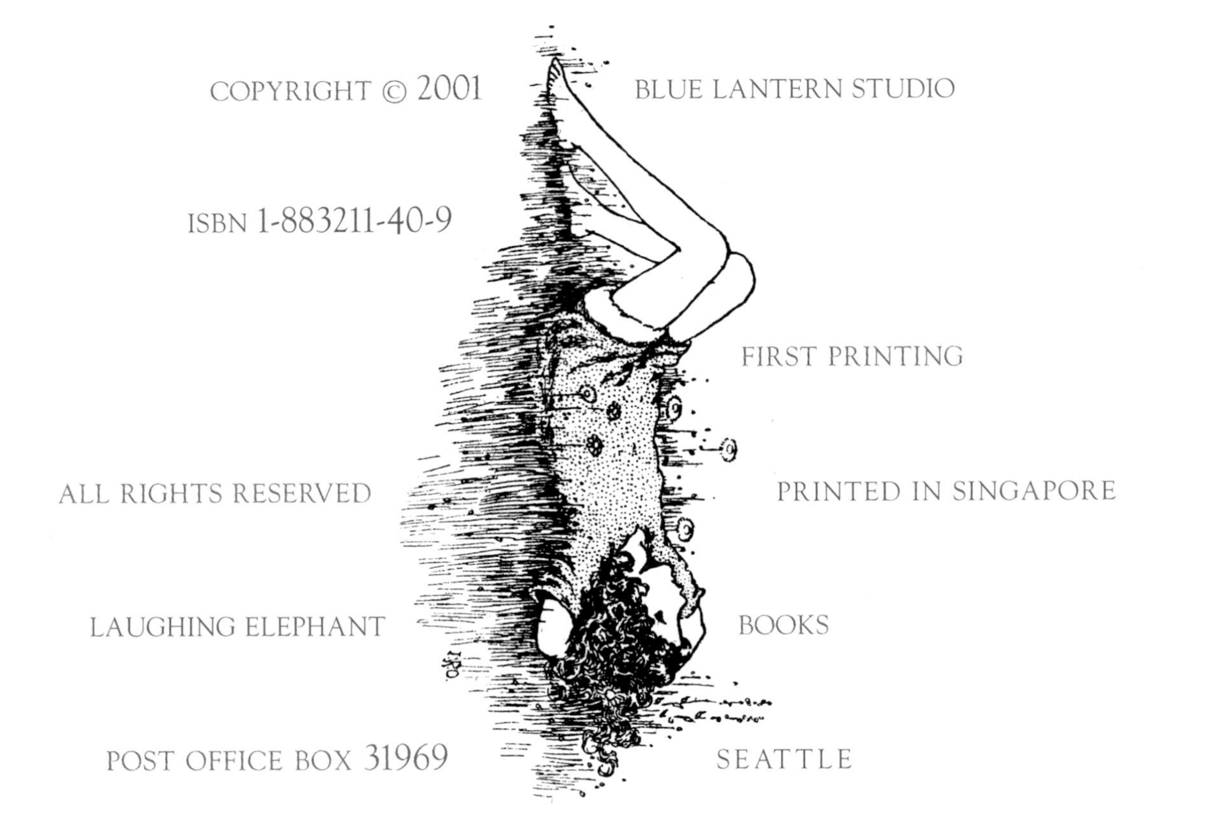

FIRST PRINTING

PRINTED IN SINGAPORE

LAUGHING ELEPHANT BOOKS

POST OFFICE BOX 31969 SEATTLE

WASHINGTON 98103

I offer this blessing of peace-the peace of drifting clouds,

and sun-filled trees;

the fresh peace of morning,

and the sweet calm of evenings;

the deep peace of a mountain lake,

and the living peace of a blooming meadow;

the healing peace of springtime;

the redolent peace of summer;

the glowing peace of autumn,

and the lovely peace that winter brings;

the peace of a buzzing garden,

Beatrice Parsons

and the calming beauty of flowers;

the sweet peace of young creatures;

the engulfing peace of moonlight,

and the peaceful gift of the stars.

PICTURE CREDITS

Dustjacket	Church, Frederic Edwin (1826-1900). "Above the Clouds at Sunrise," 1849 oil on canvas. Courtesy of theWarner Collection of Gulf States Paper Corporation, Tuscaloosa, Alabama.
Front Cover	Robinson, Frederick Cayley. "Pastoral," 1923.
Endpaper	L. Taffara. From *Le Nubi Fondamentali,* 1921.
Half-Title	Lemmen, Georges. "Beach at Heist," ca. 1891.
Frontispiece	Martin, Henri-Jean-Guillaume. "Church of Labastide," n.d.
Title Page	Unknown. Magazine illustration, 1896.
Copyright	Outhwaite, Ida Rentoul. From *Blossom: A Fairy Story,* 1928.
2	Carlsen, Emil. "Moonlight," 1913.
3	Eugen, Prins. "Molnet," 1896.
4	Rose, Guy. "The Oak," 1916.
5	Rousseau, Théodore. "Under the Birches, Evening," (Detail) 1842.
6	Gutmann, Bernhard. "Elms at Sunrise," 1913.
7	Friedrich, Caspar David. "Morning in the Mountains," (Detail) 1822.
8	Goodwin, Albert. "Fireflies, Trinidad," 1907.
9	Degouve de Nuncques, William. "Nocturne au Parc royal de Bruxelles," 1897.
10	Homer, Winslow. "An October Day," 1889.
11	Grimshaw, Atkinson. "Nab Scar" (Detail) n.d.
12	Didier-Pouget, William. "Field of Heather," n.d.
13	Gamble, John. "Joyous Spring," n.d.
14	Garber, Daniel. "Springtime in the Village," 1917.
15	Baumann, Gustave. "Cholla and Sahuaro," 1924.
16	Henry, Edward Lamson. "Forty Winks," ca. 1880.
17	Innes, George. "September Afternoon," 1887.
18	Brown, William Mason. "Autumn," n.d.
19	Martin, Henri. "Sous la Pergola", n.d.
20	Harris, Lauren. "Winter Woodland," ca. 1915.
21	Palmer, Walter Launt. "Snowy Landscape," n.d.
22	Butler, Mildred Anne. "A Window at Kilmurray," n.d.

PICTURE CREDITS

23	Parsons, Beatrice. "Rock Garden, The Crossways, Falmouth," n.d.
24	Heade, Martin Johnson. "Magnolias on Gold Velvet," ca. 1890.
25	Gulley, Catherine E. "Memories," 1924.
26	Detmold, E.J. From *The Book of Baby Pets,* ca. 1915.
27	Frieseke, Frederick Carl. "Girl With Pet Rabbit," n.d.
28	Simmons, Edward Emerson. "Night, St. Ives Bay," 1889.
29	Barry, C.F. "A Summer Night in a Garden," n.d.
30	Unknown. From *Exploring Space,* 1965.
31	Unknown. From *Splendour of the Heavens,* 1925.
34-35	Pellizza da volpedo, Giuseppe. "The Mirror of Life," 1895-1898.